Supplementary Material
for use with
JOHN THOMPSON'S MODERN COURSE FOR THE PIANO

JOHN THOMPSON

T0084199

First Grade
ETUDES

24 Studies for the Development of Fingers, Wrist, and Forearms.

Employs five-finger groups, broken chords, and examples in phrasing.

ISBN 978-1-5400-5663-4

EXCLUSIVELY DISTRIBUTED BY

HAL•LEONARD®

© 1939 by The Willis Music Co.
International Copyright Secured   All Rights Reserved

Visit Hal Leonard Online at
www.halleonard.com

Contact us:
Hal Leonard
7777 West Bluemound Road
Milwaukee, WI 53213
Email: info@halleonard.com

In Europe, contact:
Hal Leonard Europe Limited
42 Wigmore Street
Marylebone, London, W1U 2RN
Email: info@halleonardeurope.com

In Australia, contact:
Hal Leonard Australia Pty. Ltd.
4 Lentara Court
Cheltenham, Victoria, 3192 Australia
Email: info@halleonard.com.au

PREFACE

THIS book is intended to lay a foundation in technique for the FIRST GRADE piano student. It is also designed to promote reading. The author has kept in mind constantly the fact that all examples, even technical exercises, must be tuneful if the young pupil's interest is to be retained.

Only elementary pianistic figures have been employed, built for the most part on five-finger groups (the fore-runner of the scale) and broken triads (preparation for extended arpeggios to follow later on). Properly used, the book becomes at once a means of developing *Independence, Strength* and *Evenness of Finger Action,* together with *Reading and Expression.* Examples in *Phrasing, Wrist Staccato* and the use of the *Forearm* have been included.

While the book is planned to supplement John Thompson's FIRST GRADE BOOK, it will be found adaptable for use in connection with any first grade method or material.

John Thompson

CONTENTS

− PRACTICE RECORD −

_____   _____
Student's Signature   Teacher's Signature

Record of Scales and Broken Chords Studied
and Grade Earned

═══ SCALES ═══

DATE		GRADE
	═══ BROKEN CHORDS ═══	

– PRACTICE RECORD –

_____   _____
Student's Signature   Teacher's Signature

Record of Scales and Broken Chords Studied
and Grade Earned

SCALES

DATE		GRADE
	= BROKEN CHORDS =	

Enjoy Fun and Training
playing
TWO-PIANO DUOS

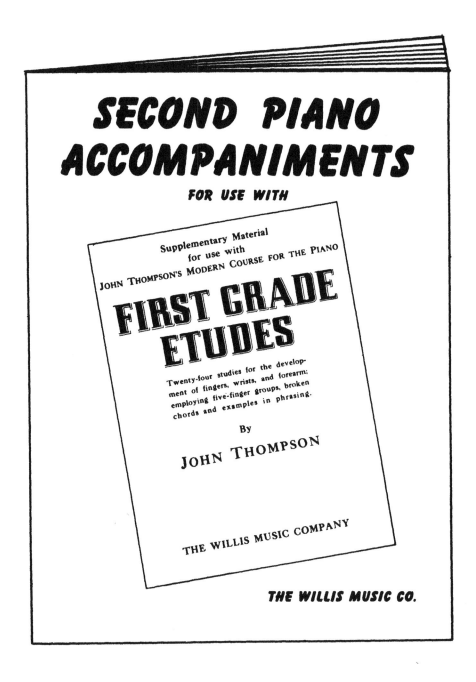

The Second Piano parts in the above book will serve to brighten the exercise period and at the same time make recital numbers of these FIRST GRADE ETUDES played by the pupil. The accompaniments are more elaborate and therefore somewhat more difficult than the etudes in the pupil's part, and should be played either by the teacher or an older pupil.

Use of Second Piano Parts is a valuable addition to any teacher's equipment.

THE WILLIS MUSIC COMPANY

Assume proper hand position.
Keep fingers nicely curved.
Use gentle, but firm touch.

The Caravan
(Finger Legato)

John Thompson

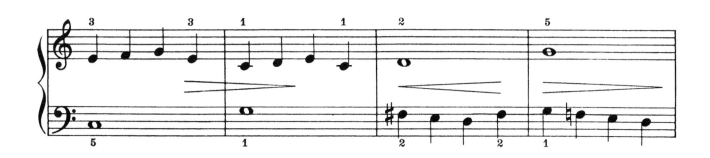

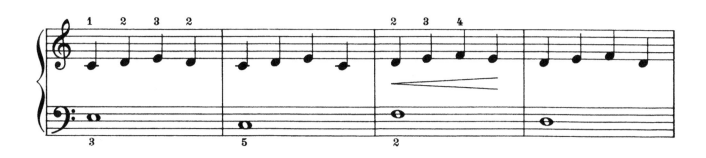

2

Sunshine and Shadow
(Broken Chords)

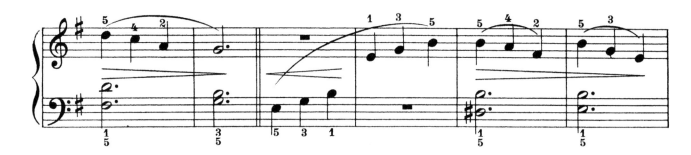

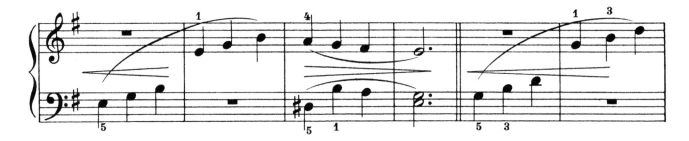

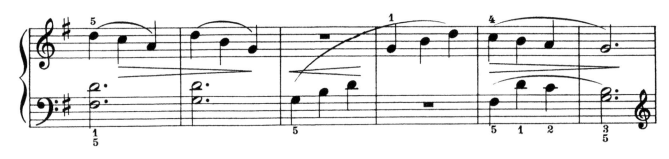

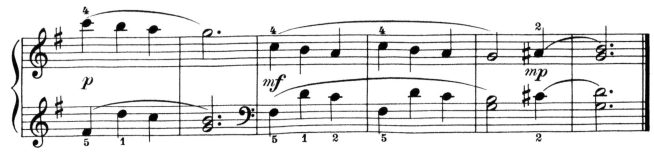

Assume proper playing position.
Raise and drop fingers with
military precision.

Ocean Tides
(Chromatic Progressions)

With animation

Cross the left hand over gracefully.
Try to make the cross-hand notes
sound like bells.

Evening Bells

(Broken Chords and Left Hand Over)

Give exact value to quarter
notes and eighth notes.
Observe all accents.

A Voyage of Discovery

(Finger Legato and Phrasing)

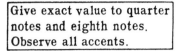

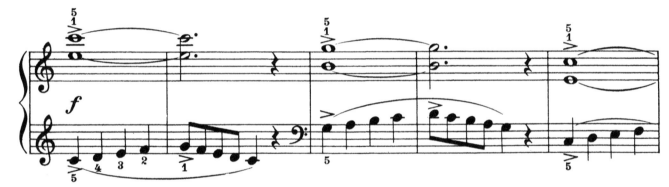

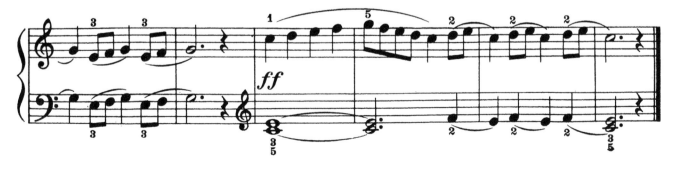

Apply smooth finger legato.
Observe the phrasing.

Windmills
(Five-Finger Groups)

Trumpeters
(Broken Chords and Accents)

Sharp distinction between legato and staccato. Rather heavy accents.

Spinning Wheel
(Right-Hand Finger Legato)

Play as smoothly as possible. Try to imitate the drone of the spinning wheel.

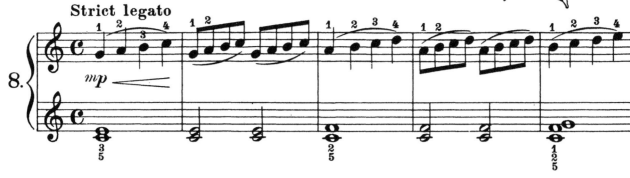

8

Sharp contrast between
legato and staccato.
Follow expression marks.

Bridge-Building
(Repeated Patterns)

Moderato

9.

Use loose, bouncing wrist attack.
Play lightly to imitate rain drops.

Raindrops
(Wrist Staccato)

Molto staccato

10.

Try to suggest the ease and
grace of a swimming fish.

Goldfish
(Scales Divided Between Both Hands)

Animato

11.

Keep an unbroken legato
and play with as much
expression as possible.

The Lonesome Pine
(Extended Broken Chords)

l. h. over

Sharp contrast between
staccato and legato.
Observe all accents.

In a Jaunting Car

(Staccato and Legato)

Cheerfully

13.

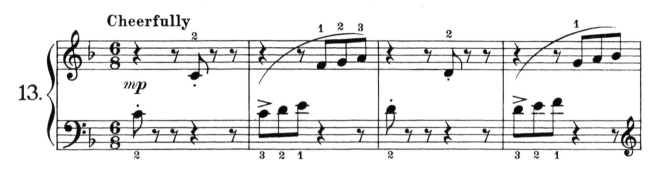

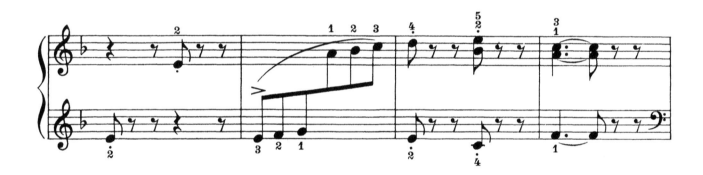

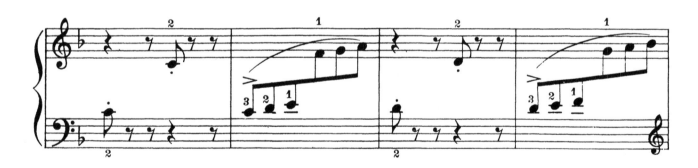

Preserve good, firm touch throughout.
Apply accents as indicated.

The Chariot Race

(Finger Independence and Evenness)

14.

Apply the drop, roll touch
to all two-note slurs.

At the Fairies' Ball
(Two-Note Phrases)

15.

Sharp phrasing

Try to scamper over the keys with the
ease and precision shown by chipmunks.

Chipmunks

(Interlocking Patterns and Trills)

Emphasize the drone effect
of the bass in imitation of
Irish bag-pipes.

On an Irish Green
(Finger Legato, Phrasing, and Melody Playing)

Sharp rhythm

19.

The Banjo
(Syncopation)

Rain Dance

(For Left Hand Alone)

Set and preserve a galloping rhythm.
Make noticeable contrast between
mf and *p*.

O'er Hill and Dale
(A Diversion in Six-Eight)

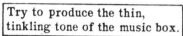

The Music Box
(Broken Chords)

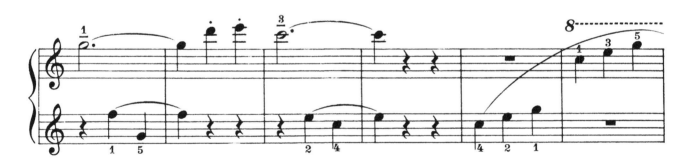

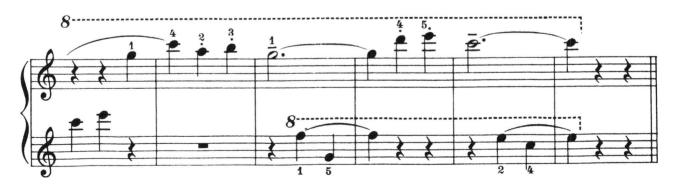

22

Twilight Song
(Forearm Chord-Playing)

ACCOMPANIMENT ALBUMS FOR USE WITH THE JOHN THOMPSON BOOKS

TEACHING LITTLE FINGERS TO PLAY ENSEMBLE

A book of accompaniments for use with John Thompson's beginner's book "Teaching Little Fingers to Play" from The Modern Course for the Piano.

Each example has two accompaniments. One makes a piano duet to be played on one piano, four hands —with teacher or parent.

The other accompaniment is more elaborate and is arranged to be played on a Second Piano by Teacher or older pupil. The Two-Piano arrangements are ideal for recital programs.

A TUNEFUL DUET ALBUM FOR THE FIRST YEAR

by John Thompson, Jr.

The material in this album is arranged for one piano, four hands. All examples are based on well-known airs and contain only notes already familiar to the Preparatory Grade Student.

The second parts are easy enough for the average parent or more advanced companion to play.

CONTENTS

An Old Nursery Tune — Samson and Delilah — Dixie — Air from "Danse Macabre" — Turkey in the Straw — Invitation to the Dance — Two Banjos — Song Without Words — Old Viennese Melody — Emperor Waltzes — La Cinquantaine

SECOND PIANO ACCOMPANIMENTS

for use with

John Thompson's
FIRST GRADE BOOK

from

The Modern Course for Piano

Many of the accompaniments are easy enough to be played by another First Grade pupil.

Others will require the teacher or older pupil.

TWO PIANO ALBUM FOR THE FIRST YEAR

A set of Second Piano accompaniments to twelve First Grade Solos from The Student Series.

Designed to be played by the teacher for ensemble training or as elaborate recital numbers.

The accompaniments are arranged for the following solos:

The Little Rocking Horse; *Ames* — Swaying Silver Birches; *Leslie* — Hoe Cake Shuffle; *Leslie* — Procession of the Seven Dwarfs; *Long* — Forest Dawn; *Thompson* — Moccasin Dance; *Long* — In the Swing; *Waldo* — Brownies Carnival; *Thompson* — Neptune's Cave; *Long* — The Story Hour; *Brooke* — Toy Ships; *Manning* — Le Tambourin; *Rameau*.

SECOND PIANO ACCOMPANIMENTS

For use with

John Thompson's
FIRST GRADE ETUDES

The etudes with their illustrations, titles and tuneful melodies have the character of little pieces. With the addition of the second parts they become readily adaptable for recital programs.

SECOND PIANO ACCOMPANIMENTS

For use with

John Thompson's
STUDIES IN STYLE

The etudes, played by the pupil, range in difficulty from Grade $1\frac{1}{2}$ to 2. The accompaniments, to be played by the teacher or more advanced student, are quite elaborate, and make ideal recital material of concert calibre when played up to tempo.

Some interesting facts about
JOHN THOMPSON

HONORS CONFERRED

DOCTOR OF MUSIC DEGREE awarded for distinguished work in furthering
Musical Education by means of his Piano Teaching Material.
FELLOW OF NATIONAL COLLEGE—Toronto, Canada.

TEACHER

DIRECTOR EMERITUS-- Conservatory of Music, Kansas City, Mo.
Former DIRECTOR PIANO DEPARTMENT- Indianapolis Conservatory of Music.
Former VICE-PRESIDENT---Leefson-Hille Conservatory, Philadelphia, Penna.

CONCERT PIANIST

John Thompson has made two European Concert Tours and numerous American
tours and has appeared as soloist with the following well-known orchestras:

London Symphony	Philadelphia Orchestra
Boston Symphony	Verdi Italian Symphony
St. Louis Symphony	Kansas City Symphony

COMPOSER

John Thompson's teaching material, in addition to its unrivalled popularity in the
United States, is widely used in CANADA, the BRITISH ISLES, AUSTRALIA,
NEW ZEALAND, countries in CENTRAL and SOUTH AMERICA and in far away
CHINA. Special editions for some of these foreign countries have been printed.
A number of his books have been transcribed and printed in Braille for the use of
the blind.

JOHN THOMPSON'S STUDENTS SERIES

A carefully selected list of Teaching Pieces, suitable for use with Books 1-a and 1-b

of

"MELODY ALL THE WAY"

Title	Composer	Key
BARNYARD FROLICS	Vivian Blackford	G.

Melody and phrasing in the right hand; broken chord accompaniment in the left.

BOGEY MAN, THE . . . . . Lois Long . . . . Am
Humoresque, with special emphasis on staccato, sudden accents and phrasing.

COBBLER, COBBLER . . . . Louise Christine Rebe . G.
Descriptive, showing tapping of cobbler's hammer. Contrast between staccato and legato.

DUTCH TWINS, THE . . . . . Willa Ward . . . . C.
Humorous Dutch dance depicting dialogue between Gretchen and Hans. Develops tonal contrast and two-note phrasing.

FOREST DAWN . . . . John Thompson . . . . . . C.
Employs broken chords and trills, describing sunrise and bird-calls.

HOE CAKE SHUFFLE . . . Charles Leslie . . . . G.
Little study in syncopation. Southern style.

IN THE SWING . . . . June Waldo . . . . C.
Melody playing in the right hand, making use of extended phrases.

LE TAMBORIN . . . . Rameau-Thompson . . . Cm
Famous old classic specially adapted for the First Grader. Contrast between staccato and legato.

LITTLE ROCKING HORSE, THE
.... J. J. Ames . . . . C.
A delightful melody, simple but most effective. The left hand is required to play two-note and three-note phrases in accompaniment.

MARCH OF THE SPOOKS
.... Edmund Haines . . . . . . Cm
Staccato in both hands. Appropriate Hallowe'en tune.

MARCHE SLAV . . . . Tschaikowsky-Thompson . . . Am
This famous melody is arranged for the right hand against a simple accompaniment in the left.

MOCCASIN DANCE . . . . . . Lois Long . . . . Am
Descriptive novelty developing melody playing and phrasing.

ON THE LEVEE . . . . June Waldo . . . . C.
Syncopated tune in the style of a Negro Spiritual.

PROCESSION OF THE SEVEN DWARFS
.... Lois Long . . . . G.
An attractive number in which both hands play in Bass Clef. Stresses staccato and accents.

SWAYING SILVER BIRCHES
.... Charles Leslie . . . . C.
Melody in the left hand. Broken chord accompaniment phrased in twos, in the right hand.

TWILIGHT LULLABY . . . Edmund Haines . . . . . . C.
Beautiful but simple melody in the right hand with a slight modern "flavor".

COVERED WAGON SUITE
.... John Thompson
Miniture suite of five First Grade pieces descriptive of important episodes in the days of 1849. Excellent material for pupils' recitals. Handsomely illustrated.

TWO PIANOS – FOUR HANDS

TOY SHIPS . . . . Mortimer Manning . . . C.
A charming recital number. Both parts lie well within First Grade.

Modern Course Supplements

CLASSICAL

Compiled and edited by Philip Low, Sonya Schumann, and Charmaine Siagian

The Classical Piano Solos series offers carefully-leveled, original piano works from Baroque to the early 20th century, featuring the simplest classics in Grade 1 to concert-hall repertoire in Grade 5. The series aims to keep with the spirit of John Thompson's legendary **Modern Course** method by providing delightful lesson and recital material that will motivate and inspire.

FIRST GRADE
Features a mix of 22 well-known pieces, including several from Bartok's method (co-authored in 1913 with Reschofsky) and Burgmüller's "Arabesque," as well as lesser-known gems by composers like Melanie Bonis, Vincent d'Indy, and Daniel Turk. Also includes two bonus pieces - by Gurlitt and Schmitt respectively - that have been adapted so that the beginning student can immediately start playing the classical repertoire.
00119738 ....$6.99

SECOND GRADE
22 original pieces from the masters! Features a mix of well-known pieces such as Petzold's "Minuet in G Major" from the Anna Magdelena Notebook, Schumann's "Soldier's March," and Beethoven's "Ecossaise in G Major," as well as lesser-known gems like d'Indy's modern "Three-Finger Partita" and Rebikov's ominous "Limping Witch Lurking in the Woods."
00119739 ....$6.99

THIRD GRADE
20 original pieces from the masters! Features a mix of well-known pieces such as Burgmüller's "Ballade" and Rebikov's "Playing Soldiers," as well as lesser-known gems like CPE Bach's "Presto" – a fast, motivating recital piece; and the lovely, lyrical "Piece Romantique" by Cecile Chaminade.
00119740 ....$7.99

FOURTH GRADE
18 original pieces from the masters! Features a mix of well-known pieces including Grieg's "Arietta" and Chopin's "Prelude in E Minor," as well as lesser-known, yet equally effective works by Teresa Carreno ("Berceuse"), Vladimir Rebikov ("The Music Lesson"), and Theodor Kullak ("The Ghost in the Fireplace").
00119741 ....$7.99

FIFTH GRADE
19 original pieces from the masters! Grade 5 features a mix of well-known pieces such as Beethoven's "Moonlight" sonata (1st mvmt) and Rachmaninoff's famous C-sharp prelude, as well as lesser-known gems from Samuel Coleridge-Taylor ("They Will Not Lend Me a Child"), Anatoly Lyadov ("Prelude in B Minor"), and Rameau ("Les niais de Sologne"). All four main periods are represented.
00119742 ....$8.99

Prices, contents, and availability subject to change without notice.

POPULAR

Arranged by Glenda Austin, Eric Baumgartner, and Carolyn Miller

These supplementary songbooks are loaded with great songs – pop hits, Broadway and movie themes, and more! Each book correlates with a grade in **Modern Course for the Piano**, and can be used as supplementary material with any piano method.

FIRST GRADE
12 songs: Edelweiss • Fly Me to the Moon • Go the Distance • It's a Small World • Let's Go Fly a Kite • Love Me Tender • Oh, What a Beautiful Mornin' • The Rainbow Connection • This Is It • What the World Needs Now Is Love • You Are My Sunshine • You'll Be in My Heart.
00416707 Book/Audio...$12.99
00416691 Book Only...$7.99

SECOND GRADE
11 songs: The Addams Family Theme • Alley Cat • Do-Re-Mi • I Could Have Danced All Night • The Masterpiece • Memory • My Heart Will Go On • Raiders March • Nadia's Theme • Sway • A Time for Us.
00416708 Book/Audio...$12.99
00416692 Book Only...$7.99

THIRD GRADE
10 songs: Beauty and the Beast • Bibbidi-Bobbidi-Boo • Castle on a Cloud • Climb Ev'ry Mountain • Getting to Know You • The Glory of Love • Goodnight, My Someone • Medley from *The Phantom of the Opera* • Tomorrow • Yesterday.
00416709 Book/Audio...$12.99
00416693 Book Only...$7.99

FOURTH GRADE
10 all-time favorites: Chariots of Fire • Endless Love • Imagine • Mission: Impossible Theme • Moon River • On Broadway • Seasons of Love • Somewhere Out There • Till There Was You • A Whole New World.
00416710 Book/Audio...$12.99
00416694 Book Only...$7.99

FIFTH GRADE
10 great arrangements: Be Our Guest • Cabaret • Georgia on My Mind • In the Mood • Let It Be • Linus and Lucy • Puttin' On the Ritz • Under the Sea • The Way You Look Tonight • What a Wonderful World.
00416711 Book/Audio...$14.99
00416695 Book Only...$9.99

EXCLUSIVELY DISTRIBUTED BY

WILLIS MUSIC   HAL•LEONARD®

www.willispianomusic.com